THE DAKOTA
APARTMENTS
A Pictorial History of New York's Legendary Landmark

Written & Designed
by

Copyright 2015
by The Cardinals

All Rights Reserved. No part of this publication may be reproduced, stored in a retrieval system, or transmitted in any form or by any means, electronic, email, photocopying, recording, scanning, or otherwise, without the prior written permission of the Publisher. The content of this book is of a historical, educational, and newsworthy nature, and is made available in the name of the public interest. Considering the purpose and character of the transformative use of the text and photos in creating a new work, the Publisher is confident that their use does not directly affect and/or compete with any potential claimant's business or potential for income. The Publishers are confident that there is no part of this book that is in violation of, or infringes upon, anyone's copyrights, trademarks, licensing, privacy, or postmortem publicity rights.

Limit of Liability/Disclaimer of Warranty: While the Publishers and the Author(s) have used their best efforts in preparing this book, they make no representations or warranties with respect to the accuracy or completeness of the contents of this book and specifically disclaim any implied warranties of merchantability or fitness for a particular purpose. Neither the Publisher nor the Author(s) shall be liable for any loss of profit or any other commercial damages, including, but not limited to, special, incidental, consequential, or other damages.

All reasonable effort has been made to contact the photographers and copyright owners of all images printed in this publication. Any omissions or errors are inadvertent and will be corrected in subsequent editions, provided written notification is sent to the Publisher. Many of the images in this book are transformative works and are protected by their own copyrights as well as the overall copyright protecting the contents of this book.

The Campfire Network publishes its books in a variety of formats. Some content that appears in print may not be available in electronic books, and vice versa. The content of this book was generated during scholarly research on architectural history.

For information on any books published by the Campfire Network & Campfire Publishing, or for bulk & wholesale orders, or to schedule interviews with any of the Authors, please contact Cardinal@CampfireNetwork.com.

Acknowledgments & Dedication

A book of this sort can rarely be completed without the kind assistance of numerous generous individuals. Over the course of the time we have spent researching the Dakota we have had the genuine pleasure of interacting, and sometimes befriending, an assortment of wonderful people who shared our enthusiasm for the Dakota and were kind enough to assist us in a variety of ways. Many took the time to answer a few simple questions. Many engaged us in long and fruitful conversations about the history and architecture of the Dakota. Most of all, they all shared their memories with us. First and foremost we want to thank Mr. Stephen Birmingham for taking the time to share his bounty of knowledge; much of which can be found in his wonderful 1979 book "Life at the Dakota." Architectural Historian Barry Lewis was an absolute treasure-trove of incredible information. We have been fortunate enough to communicate with numerous present and former Dakota residents. Above all others, we would like to shine a grateful light upon them. We offer our sincerest thanks to Rex Reed, Del Brownlee, Tony Victoria, Albert Maysles, and Lauren Bacall for being greathearted and responsive to our inquirees. A special thank you to Andrew Alpern who was so impressed with our research many years ago, and inspired by our book "The Dakota Scrapbook" (published, 2014) that a collaboration between he and I on a hardcover Dakota book had ensued. Thank you to Brian T. Silak for allowing us to reprint his photo of Roberta Flack, and for Steven Sater for kind permission to reprint his photo. We also want to acknowledge our friends Neil McEachern, Jack Perry, Rachel Galvin, Robert Harper, Catherine Harper, Gerhard Bohrer, Servi Stevens, and Steve Silberberg for their invaluable feedback. This book could not be completed without the love and support of D.C. Blackbird. We want to extend a special thank you to Richie Ornstein and Joe Franklin. Joe was indeed the King of Nostalgia and shall always be an important part of New York's history. If it were not for Joe we may never have been able to take those first steps into the Dakota that we dreamed about throughout our lives. We shall never forget him and for all he had done for us. And a very special thank you to "Uncle Frank Rose," the great Magician and Musician who ran the legendary Circle Magic Shop on Broadway.

Dedicated to:
Jekyll, Autumn, Bridgette and D.C.B.

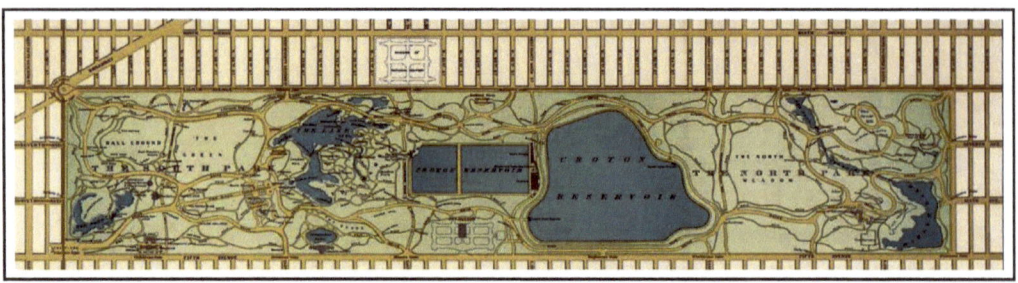

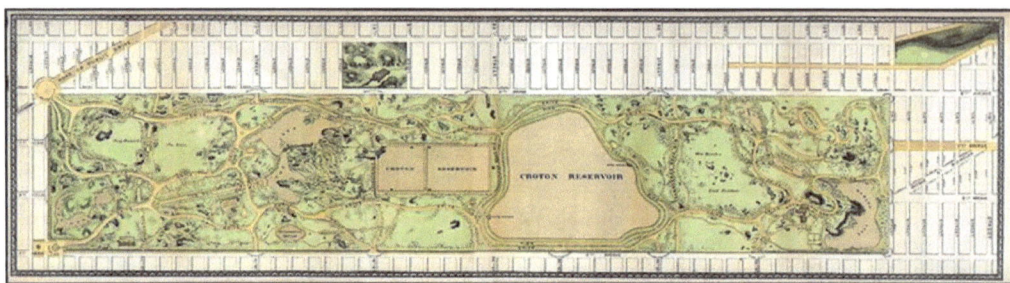

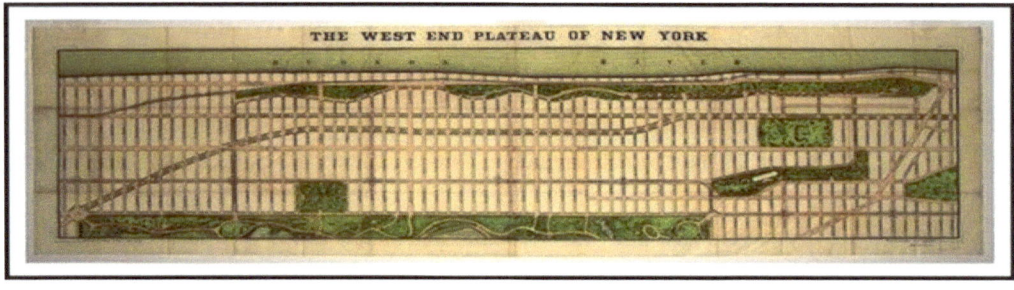

THE WEST END PLATEAU OF NEW YORK

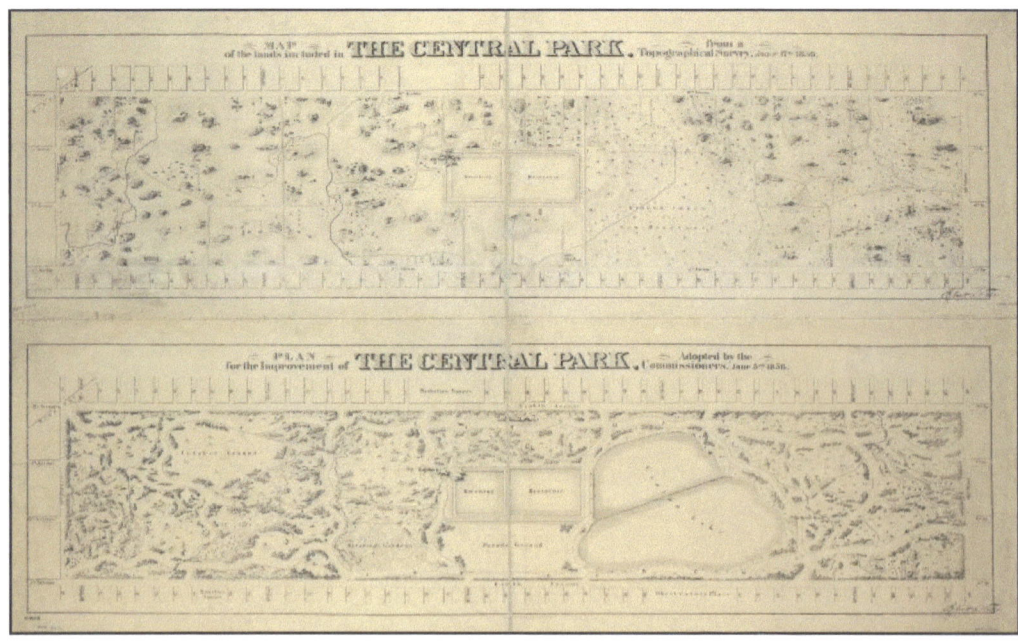

Contents

Introduction

Chapter 1:   View from the East
Chapter 2:   View from the Southeast
Chapter 3:   View from the South
Chapter 4:   View from the West
Chapter 5:   View from Above
Chapter 6:   The Moat
Chapter 7:   View from Central Park
Chapter 8:   View from Roof
Chapter 9:   Floor Plans
Chapter 10: Private Restaurant
Chapter 11: Courtyard
Chapter 12: Apartments
Chapter 13: Edward Clark
Chapter 14: Isaac Singer
Chapter 15: Henry Hardenbergh
Chapter 16: Residents

6

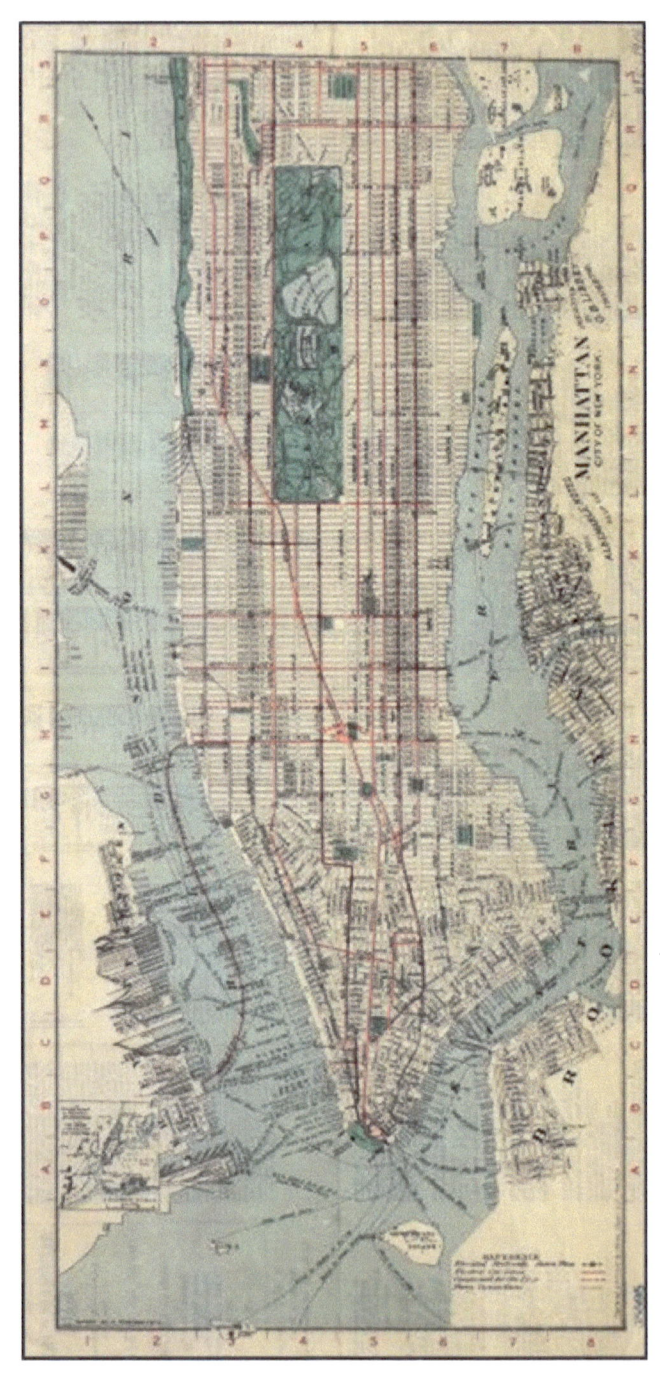

THE DAKOTA

INTRODUCTION

The Dakota is one of the most beautiful and legendary residential buildings in New York City. It was built by Edward Clark who was partners with Isaac Singer, the inventor of the Singer Sewing Machine. Mr. Clark was already a well-known and respected real estate developer when he purchased the land on West 72nd Street in 1879 where the Dakota would be built between 1880-1884 based on architectural designs by Henry Janeway Hardenbergh. Though he did not live to see it completed, Edward Clark intended to live in a 6th floor apartment in order to set the example to wealthy individuals in New York that they could comfortably live in a "French Flat" as opposed to the mansions that they lived in up until that time. The Dakota set a new standard for luxury living in America. Nothing of its caliber had ever existed as a residence before and it quickly leased all of its apartments without having to advertise. Because of its unique beauty, the Dakota has always been a popular subject of illustrations and photographs. We share many of them here for your enjoyment, in hopes that you will appreciate the Dakota as much as we do.

The Cardinals
Investigative Historians

A PICTORIAL HISTORY

One
VIEW FROM THE EAST

1885 illustration of the Dakota that accompanied an article in the Real Estate Record and Builders Guide.

1903 photo of the Dakota taken from inside Central Park.

A PICTORIAL HISTORY

10

1895 photo of the Dakota taken from the unpaved Terrace Drive inside Central Park.

THE DAKOTA

1886 photo of the Dakota taken from inside Central Park.

A PICTORIAL HISTORY

1927 photo of the Dakota taken from inside Central Park with approaching vehicles.

THE DAKOTA

1929 photo of the Dakota taken from inside Central Park.

A PICTORIAL HISTORY

East elevation. Historic American Buildings Survey, 1965.

THE DAKOTA

The upper stories of the Dakota can be seen from within Central Park. The flagpole in the center is actually secured inside the top portion of the pyramidal structure beneath it.

A PICTORIAL HISTORY

Two
View from the Southeast

View of the Dakota's southeast corner taken from within the walls of Central Park.

THE DAKOTA

1912 photo of the east side of the Dakota, facing Central Park. On the right is The Langham apartment building that was completed in 1907. Originally the property could not be sold to anyone who would construct a building taller than the Dakota. After difficulty selling the property that provision was removed. Automobiles are parked along West 72nd Street in front of the Dakota.

A PICTORIAL HISTORY

Three
View from the South

Detailed 1885 illustration of the Dakota that accompanied an article in the Sanitary Engineer.

1885 illustration by Hughes Hawley of the Dakota from the southeast.

A PICTORIAL HISTORY

View of the Dakota's south side, and part of the east side, taken from across Eighth Avenue, circa 1890.

View of the Dakota from the southeast.

A PICTORIAL HISTORY

1882 illustration for the Evening World showing the south side of the Dakota with shacks and a farm with goats and chickens in the foreground.

THE DAKOTA

South (front) facade. Historic American Buildings Survey, 1965.

A PICTORIAL HISTORY

24

South entrance detail. Historic American Buildings Survey, 1965. (colorized)

THE DAKOTA

Extreme closeup of the 72nd Street entry with the original decorative gate. This entry was used by pedestrians and carriages.

Four
View from the West

This photo taken from West 72nd Street shows the west side of the Dakota and Clark Park. On the left are the row houses that Henry Janeway Hardenbergh designed for Edward Clark who owned a good portion of the real estate property around the Dakota. The electric plant that was installed underground was sufficient to offer electricity to the Dakota and surrounding buildings.

THE DAKOTA

View from the southwest corner of the Dakota. There is a gate along the sidewalk, to the left of the ivy, that offered residents access to Clark Park. Curiously, the "back" of the Dakota was not nearly as ornate as the sides that were seen by the street. Perhaps Clark and Hardenbergh expected another building to eventually be built next to it, with perhaps a narrow alleyway remaining. What confuses this assumption is that Clark owned the property to the west, placed boilers underground, and used it as a park for residents. The west side of the building is simply adorned with red brick and window awnings.

A PICTORIAL HISTORY

Five
VIEW FROM ABOVE

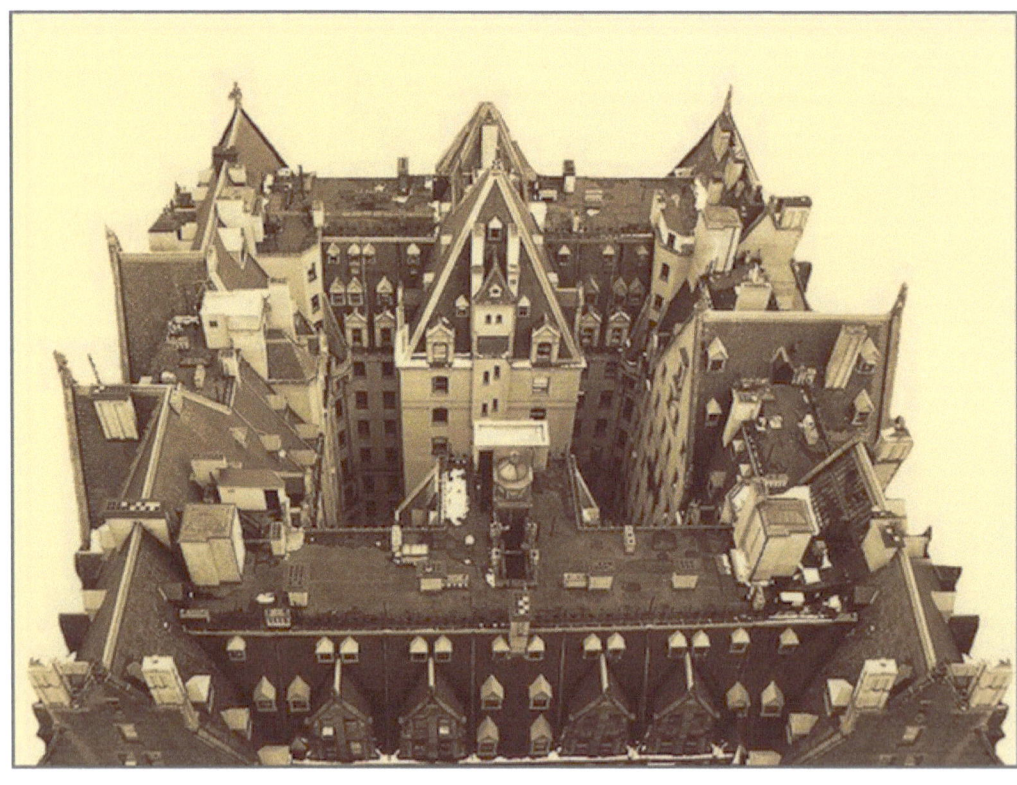

There is evidence and references to a planned rooftop garden from its earliest days. As a result, since its completion, the Dakota's roof has been easily accessed and enjoyed by residents. While visiting New York in 1891 Pyotr Ilyich Tchaikovsky was given a tour of the roof by his host Gustav Schirmer following a dinner party in Schirmer's Dakota apartment.

THE DAKOTA

The Dakota's roof has been described as looking down upon a miniature European village, with its gables, pyramids, towers, chimneys and windows of various shapes and sizes. (photo courtesy of Thomas Cathey)

A PICTORIAL HISTORY

Six
The Moat

This photo shows the elaborate guard rail that runs along the dry moat on the east facade of the Dakota. In addition to adding an imposing allure, the dry moat was designed for the benefit of security, but also to allow light to penetrate through the windows of the basement below. The decorative stone balcony belongs to the ground-floor apartment in the center of the building.

The dry moat runs along the south, east and north sides of the Dakota, with stone bridges that need to be traversed in order to gain entry to the building. This photo of the bearded face and accompanying sea creatures was taken as part of the Historic American Buildings Survey.

A PICTORIAL HISTORY

Seven
View from Central Park

"Sleighing in Central Park" engraving by W.P. Snyder, circa 1886.

"A view in Central Park, showing Dakota Flats," circa 1891. Engravers: Flintoff & Breslin.

Etching of the Dakota apartments with Central Park in the foreground, by Charles F. Mielatz (1864-1919)

THE DAKOTA

Pen and ink sketch of the Dakota from behind a rock, circa 1885, by Eliza Pratt Greatorex (1819 – 1897)

A PICTORIAL HISTORY

Circa 1900 photo taken from Terrace Drive. In the distance is the statue of Daniel Webster and the Dakota.

1908 postcard: Central Park, Statute of Daniel Webster. Sculptor: Thomas Ball (1819-1911). Material: Bronze on granite base. Presented by: Gordon W. Burnham, 1876.

A PICTORIAL HISTORY

This photo shows Central Park in the foreground with the Dakota on the far left. To its right is the Langham

THE DAKOTA

On the far right of this photo, within Central Park, surrounded by trees, is Belvedere Castle.

A PICTORIAL HISTORY

Vintage colorized postcard showing the Dakota and the Hotel Majestic with Central Park's lake and the Bow Bridge in the foreground.

THE DAKOTA

Circa 1897 by C.F. Theodore Kreh.

A PICTORIAL HISTORY

Central Park offered beautiful views of the Dakota and vice versa. Interestingly, the servants who resided in the Dakota's attic rooms had better views of Centrak Park than many of the residents.

Spring view of the Dakota from the lake in Central Park, circa 1880.

A PICTORIAL HISTORY

Photos of the Upper West Side as seen from Central Park.

THE DAKOTA

View from Central Park, circa 1930. At this time the Hotel Majestic to the immediate south of the Dakota was replaced by the Art Deco-style Majestic Apartments with two towers facing Central Park. Behind it can be seen The Oliver Cromwell, a 30-story Tower designed by architect Emery Roth and completed in 1927.

Early 20th century photo of Central Park from the north side of the reservoir. The Dakota and other buildings along Central Park West are in the distance.

THE DAKOTA

Within 50 years of the Dakota's completion the Upper West Side became one of the most popular urban neighborhoods in the world.

A PICTORIAL HISTORY

This early 20th century photo taken from the Sheep Meadow in Central Park shows the Dakota and surrounding luxury buildings.

THE DAKOTA

The beautiful design of the Dakota created an attractive backdrop against the naturescape of Central Park.

A breathtaking photo of ice skaters on the lake in Central Park with the regal Dakota in the distance.

THE DAKOTA

Central Park was designed to be enjoyed by all New Yorkers - wealthy and poor, men and women.

A PICTORIAL HISTORY

These photos show people enjoying the frozen pond in Central

THE DAKOTA

To the south of the Dakota is the Hotel Majestic, designed by Alfred Zucker in 1894

A PICTORIAL HISTORY

Eight
VIEW FROM ROOF

This photo shows the westward view from the Dakota's roof. At the time, apartments on the west side of the building had a view of the Hudson River. The rest of the block between 72nd Street - 73rd Street is clearly still undeveloped. The El Train is visible along Ninth Avenue. This photo offers further proof that the legendary story of the building being called the "Dakota" - in reference to the Dakota Territory - because the Upper West Side was essentially like a prairie. Simply put, Edward Clark liked the name of America's Western states and territories. In fact, it was Mr. Clark who suggested in the 1870s (before the Dakota was constructed) that Eleventh Avenue be known as Idaho Place, Tenth Avenue as Arizona Place, Ninth Avenue as Wyoming Place, and that Eighth Avenue should be known as Montana Place.

THE DAKOTA

Looking southwest from the roof of the Dakota. The El Train can be seen on the bottom right. In the distance is the Hudson River and New Jersey.

A PICTORIAL HISTORY

This 1887 photo offers a unique southward view from the Dakota's rooftop. At the time the two-way road on the left was still known as Eighth Avenue. On April 22, 1890 the portion from 59th Street - 110th Street was renamed Central Park West. On the far left is Central Park which had been officially opened since 1873. Contrary to popular belief, the area surrounding the Dakota was not completely desolate. While still considered a rural area, it was filled with a variety of summer houses and estates, farms, shanty villages, and shacks. The beauty of the Dakota helped set the tone for the direction the neighborhood would take and further stimulated the West Side's development.

This northwestern view shows the beautiful row houses that Henry Hardenbergh designed for Edward Clark along West 73rd Street. These attractive homes helped create a neighborhood around the Dakota and encouraged other West End developers to follow their lead. In the foreground of the bottom left of this photo is green grass and a fence that encloses "Clark Park." Though designed for the enjoyment of residents, its original intention was to conceal the boilers that were in an underground room. On the bottom left is Clark and Hardenbergh's 101 West 73rd Street apartment building which still stands.

This photo shows a similair view of West 73rd Street from the Dakota's roof as it looked in 1928.

A PICTORIAL HISTORY

Taken from the roof of the Dakota in 1885, this photo shows a northward view of the Upper West Side. The large structure in the center of the frame is the first building built for the American Museum of Natural History on West 79th Street.

East side facade of the American Museum of Natural History.

THE DAKOTA

This view shows a fine view of Central Park from the 6th floor balcony of the center apartment along the east side of the Dakota. In the distance are buildings on the east side of the park and along 59th Street on the right side.

Nine

Floor Plans

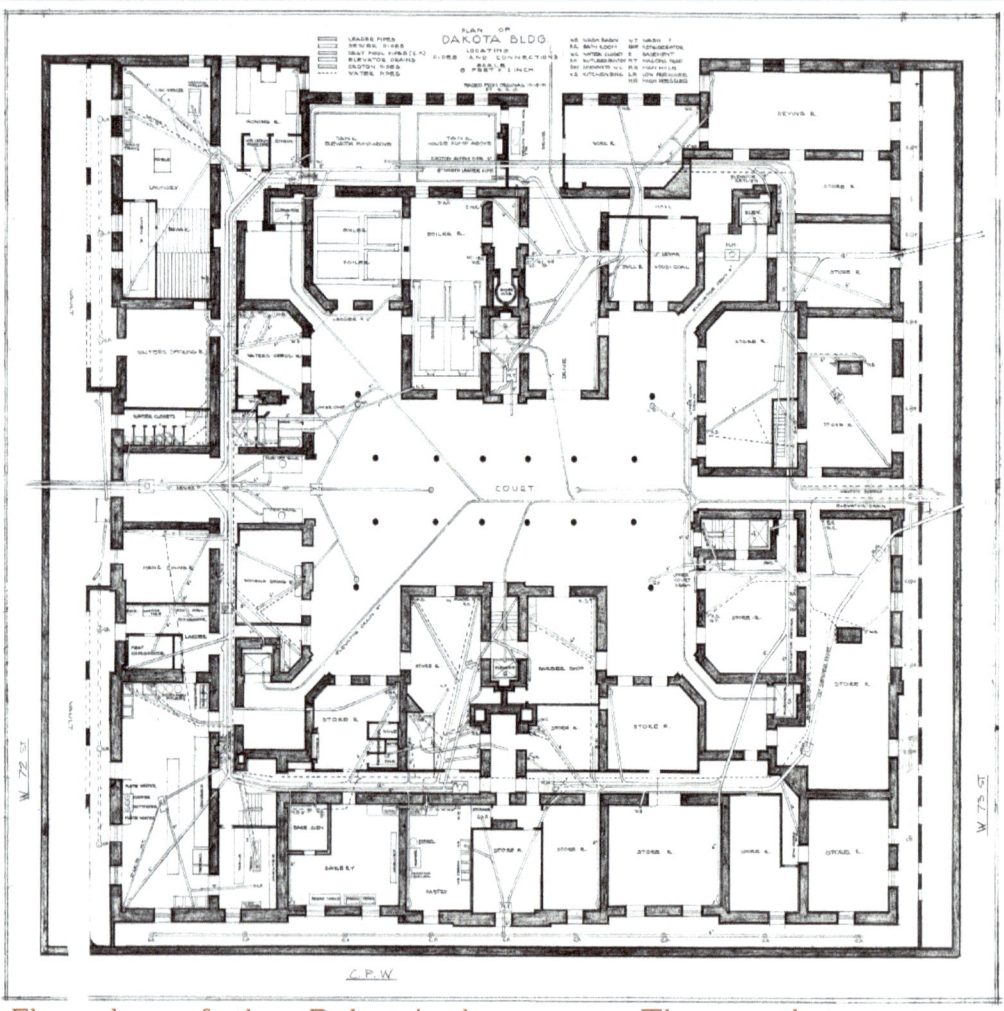

Floorplan of the Dakota's basement. The southwest corner rooms were used for laundry and ironing. There were waiters' smoking rooms, waitress' dressing rooms, separate dining rooms for male and female servants, a bakery, boiler rooms, an ice cream freezer, a barber shop, storage rooms, and more. The underground court is the same size as the one above in order to allow horses-and-carriages to easily enter for deliveries.

THE DAKOTA

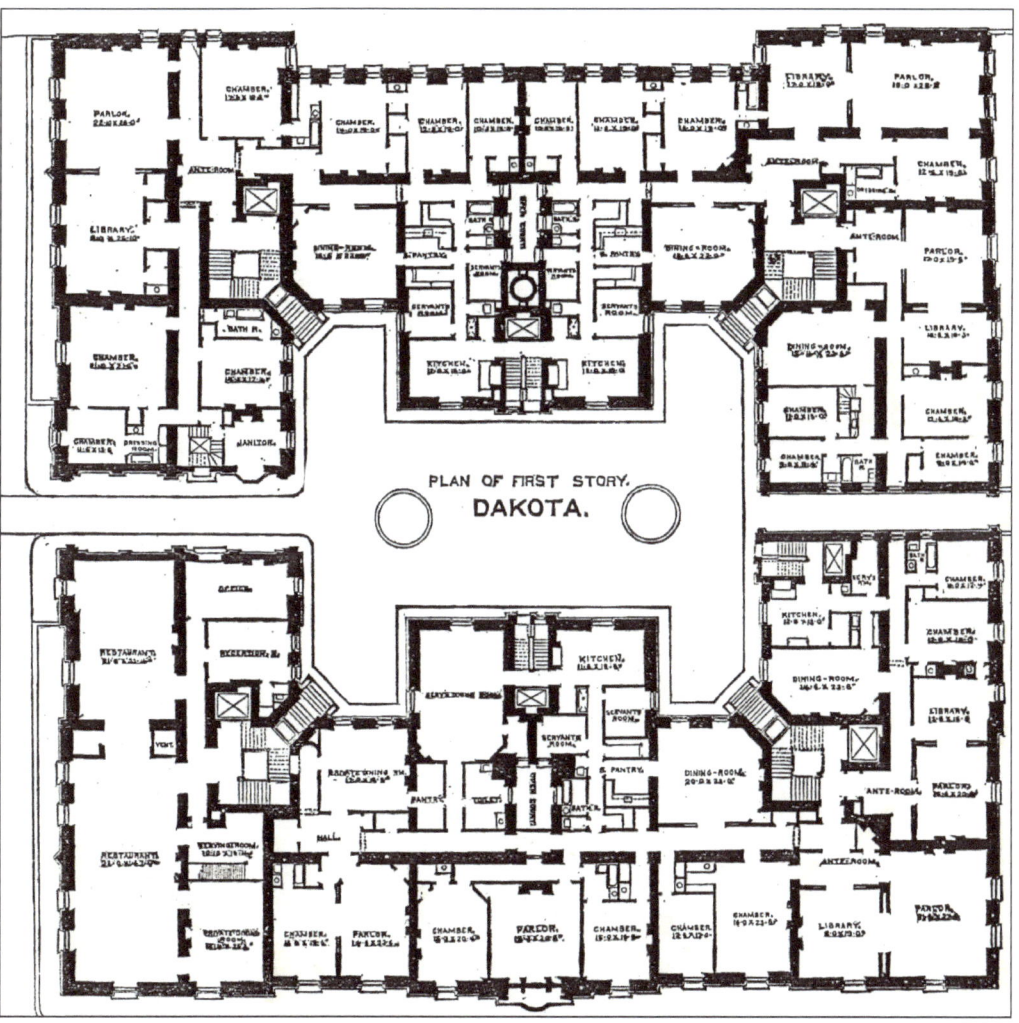

This vintage floorplan of the first (1st) floor include the north and south entries to the courtyard from the streets. The bottom left hand corner was the location of the private restaurant. In the latter part of the 20th century a portion of the apartment on the southwest corner was converted into a smaller apartment with a private entry from a specially-designed staircase. In the 1970s that apartment was owned by Gilda Radner. Its most recent well-known resident was John Madden.

A PICTORIAL HISTORY

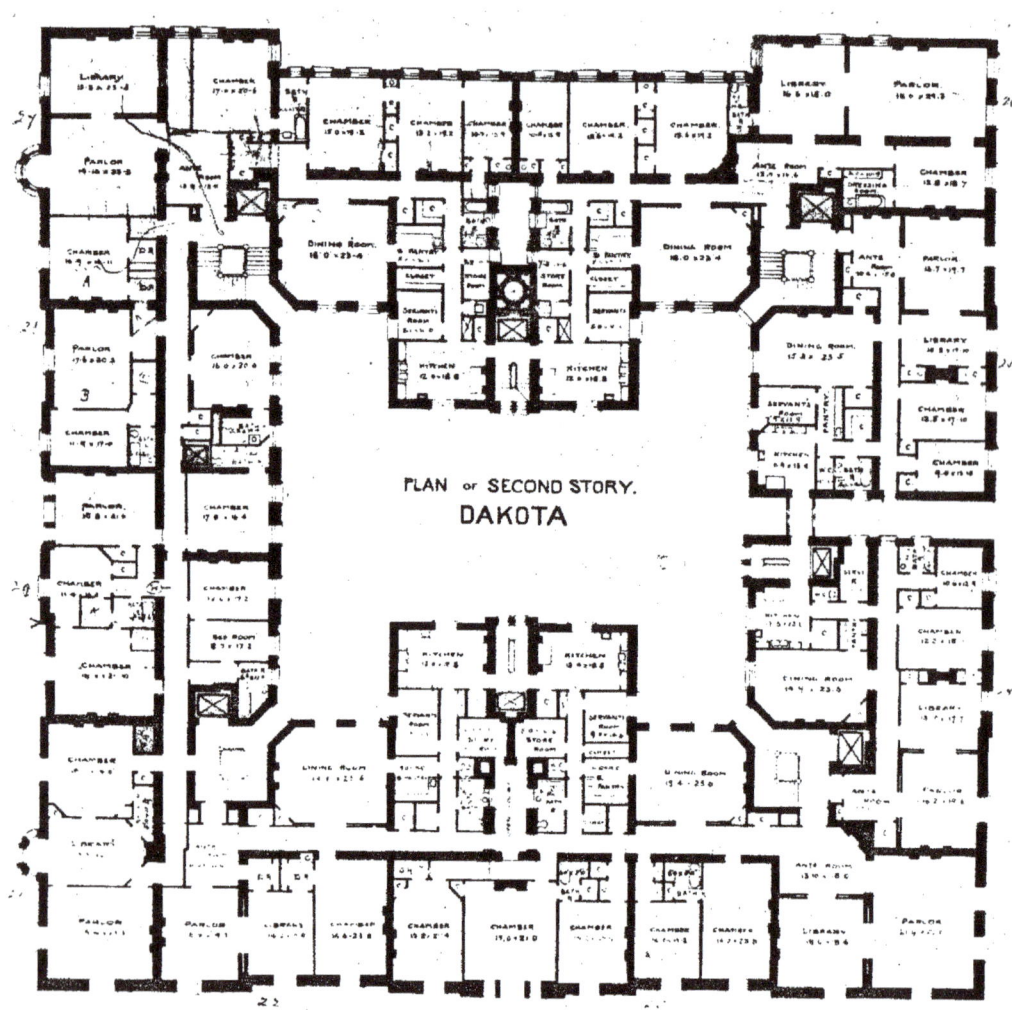

This is a vintage floorplan of the second (2nd) floor of the Dakota. In addition to large apartments that were similiar in layout to those on other floors, Hardenbergh designed smaller apartments that could be temporarily rented by Dakota residents for the use of their guests. Legend has it that whenever Edward Severin Clark came to Manhattan he preferred staying in one of the smaller guest apartments rather than in the enormous apartment originally designed for his grandfather.

THE DAKOTA

This is a vintage floorplan of the third (3rd) floor of the Dakota.

A PICTORIAL HISTORY

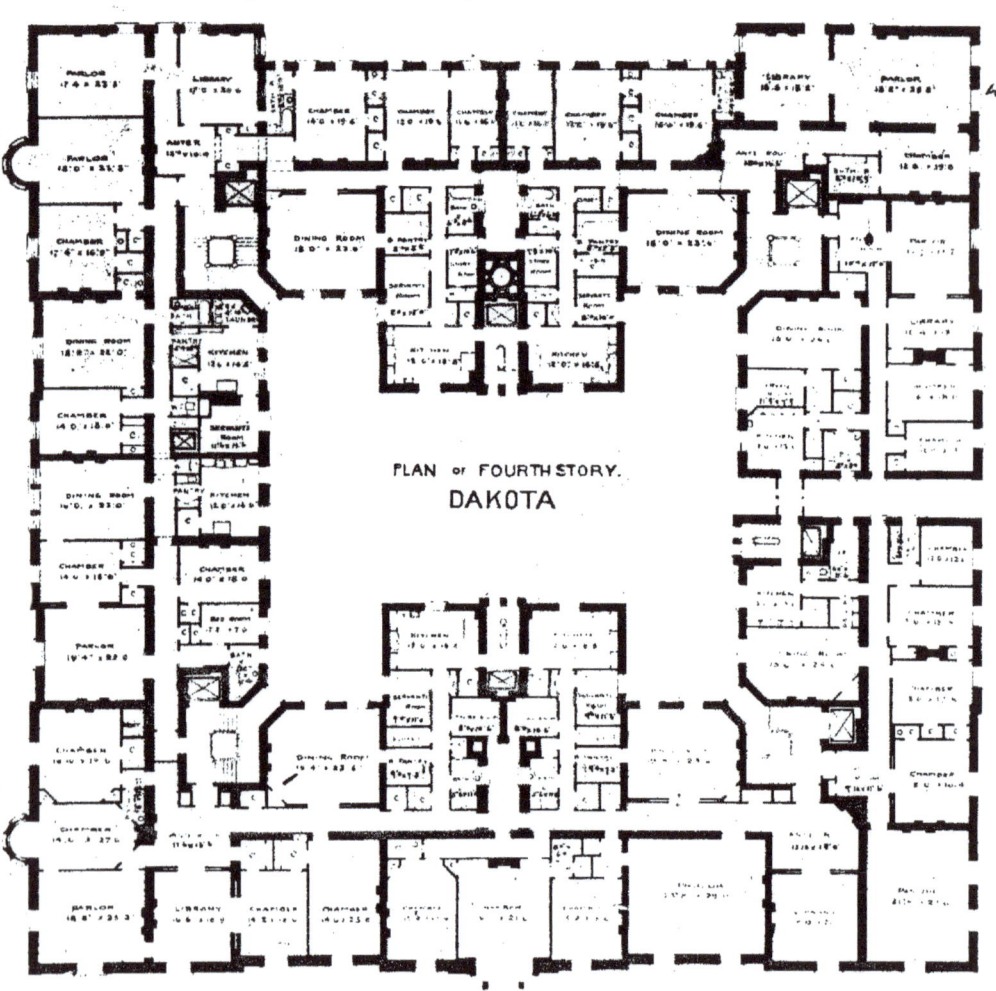

This is a vintage floorplan of the fourth (4th) floor of the Dakota. It is well-known that actress Lauren Bacall lived in the apartment on the northeast corner. She purchased the apartment from the family of operatic baritone John Brownlee.

THE DAKOTA

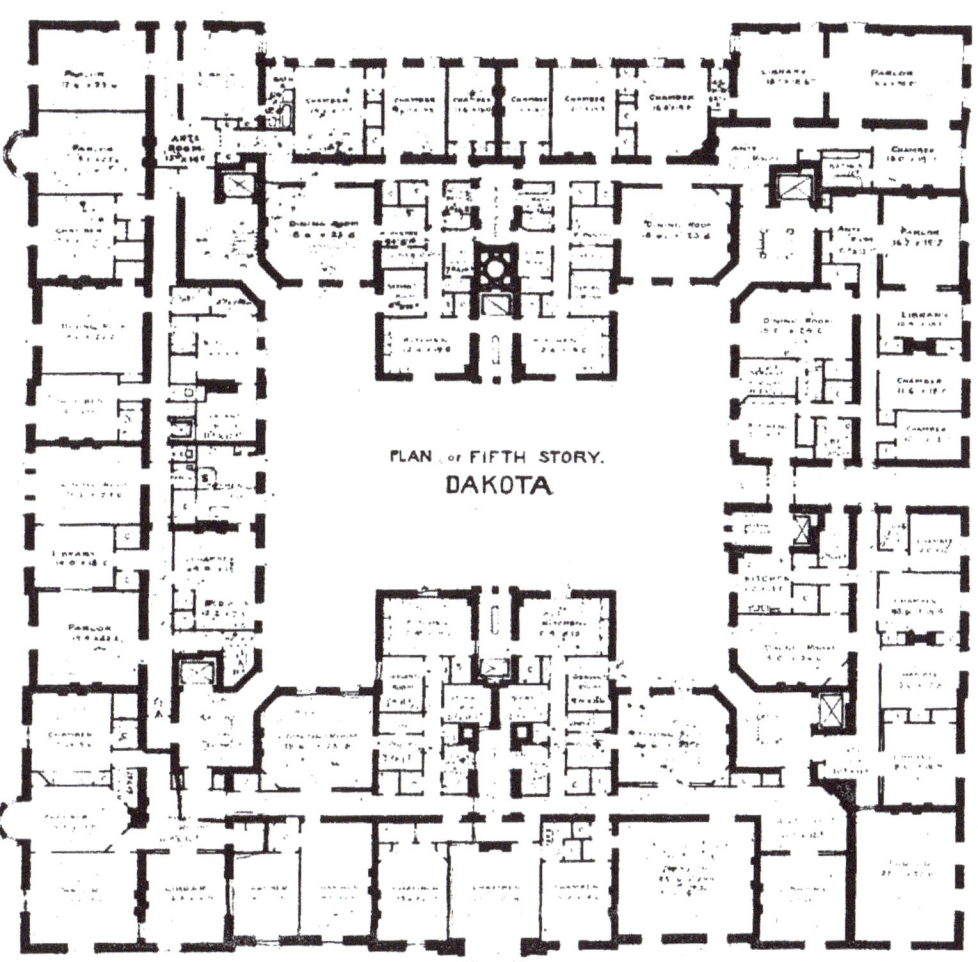

This is an original floorplan of the fifth (5th) floor of the Dakota.

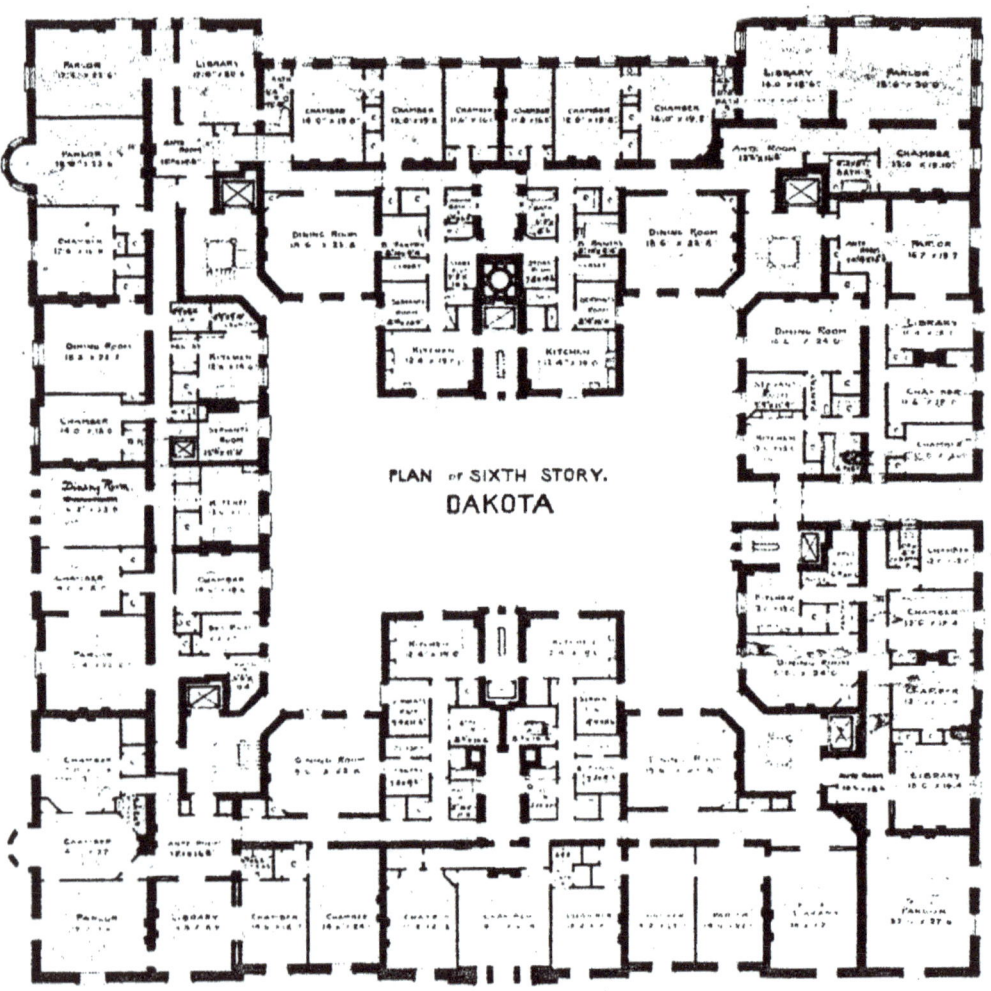

This is a vintage floorplan of the sixth (6th) floor of the Dakota. During design and construction the Dakota's owner was concerned that potential residents would not want to live on the higher floors since upper floors were typically associated with servant's quarters. As a result, he decided to set an example by living in one of the largest apartments on the floor. It included a 24 x 49 ft. long Drawing Room, along with over a dozen large chambers and wood-burning fireplaces.

THE DAKOTA

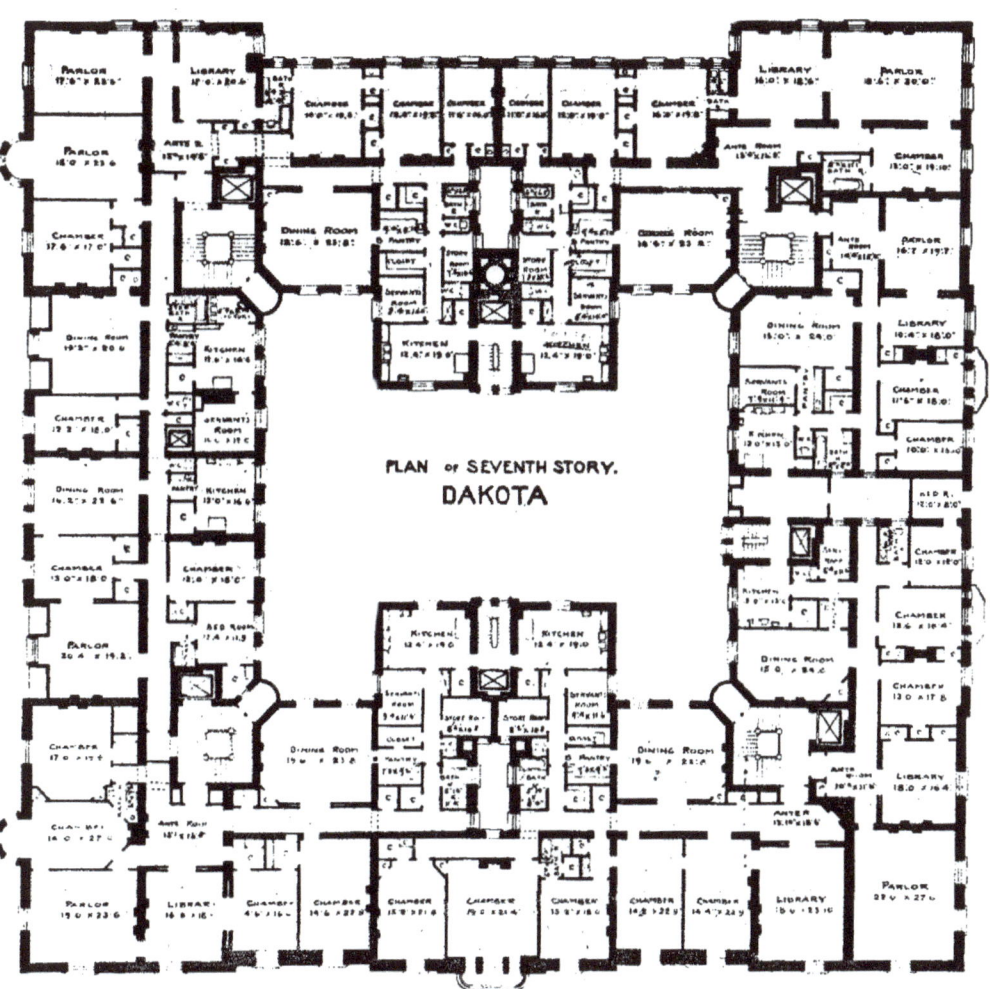

This is a vintage floorplan of the seventh (7th) floor of the Dakota. This floor offered the finest views of Central Park from apartments on the east side, as well as those on the south and north sides before the Hotel Majestic (1894) and the Langham (1905) were built. It is well-known that John Lennon and Yoko Ono purchased their first Dakota apartment on the southeast corner of the 7th floor. The apartment was previously owned by actor Robert Ryan.

A PICTORIAL HISTORY

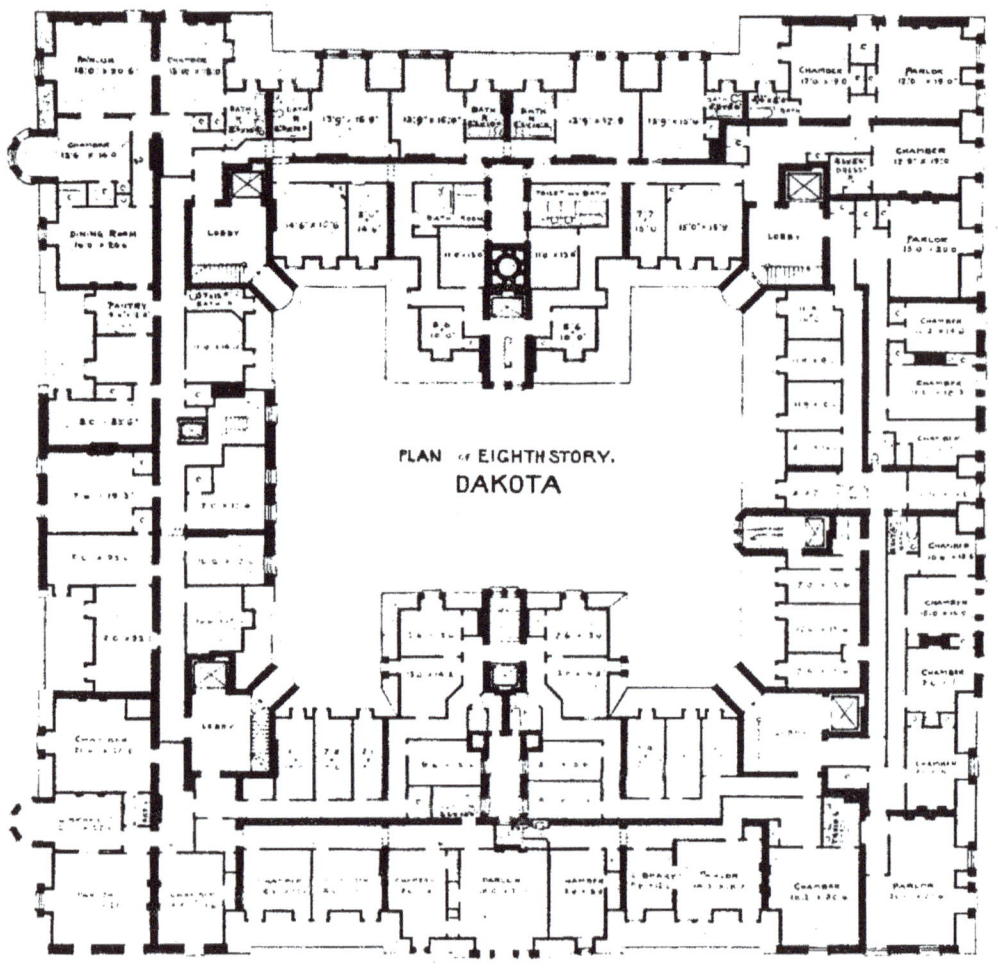

This is a vintage floorplan of the eighth (8th) floor of the Dakota. As part of the lower level of the attic, many of the small rooms were designed to be used for storage. However, Hardebergh and Clark made the decision of creating apartments in each corner that could be rented out by residents for the use of their visiting guests. It is this floor where Boris Karloff and his wife had an apartment.

THE DAKOTA

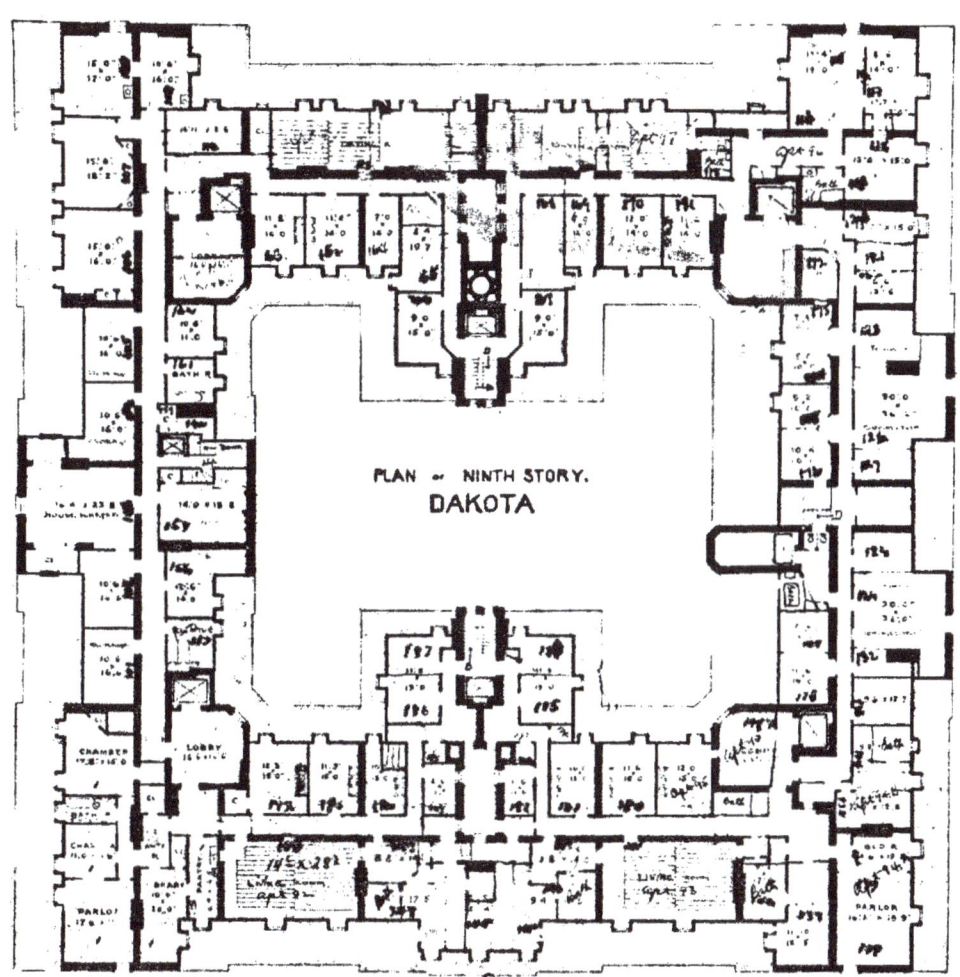

This is a vintage floorplan of the ninth (9th) floor of the Dakota. Many of the small rooms were designed for the storage of linens and other supplies used, while others were living quarters of some of the original 150 servants who worked in the building. Areas of the floor were designed as bathrooms with multiple toilets. The ninth (9th) floor contained the staircases to acces the roof.

A PICTORIAL HISTORY

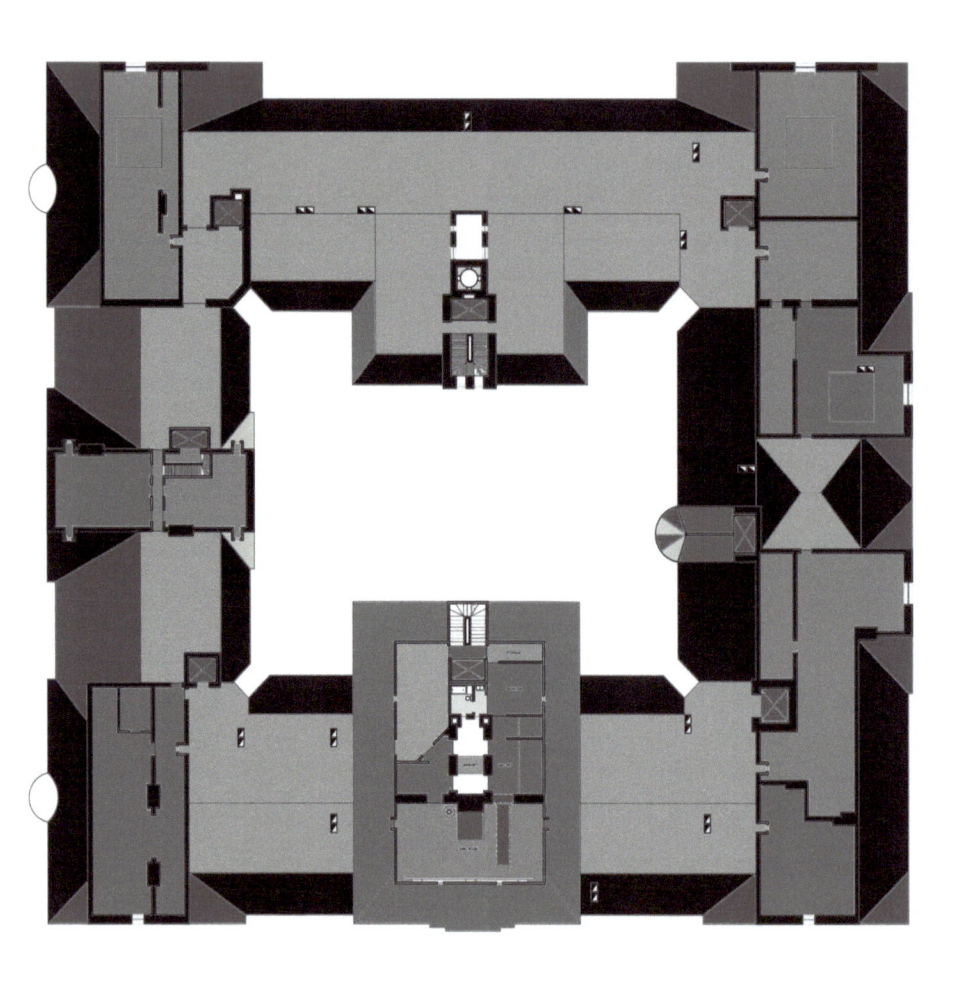

This plan of the Dakota's rooftop shows the location of the service and residential elevators shafts. The roof was accessed by staircases from the top floor of the attic. In the center of the east side of the building is a pyramid-shaped apartment designed by designer, artist and sculptor Ward Bennett. The rooms were originally meant for storage, and were then converted as sleeping quarters for servants.

THE DAKOTA

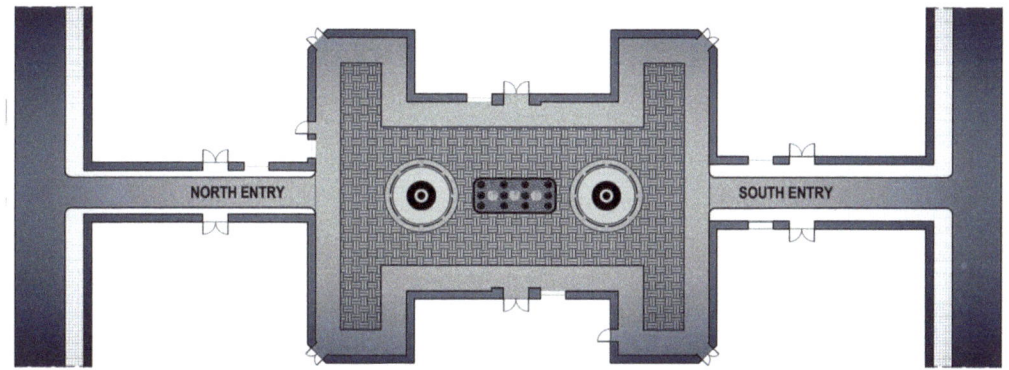

This diagram above shows the layout of the courtyard. The south entry leads out onto West 72nd Street and has always been the main entry for residents and their guests. The north entry leads out onto West 73rd Street. The security gate there has been locked and inaccesible for decades. It was originally planned to be an entry for many of the servants who worked in the building. When that proved to be inconvenient, the servants strictly entered through the building's basement from the alley along the west side of the building.

The above diagram shows the doors on each corner that lead to the individual lobbies. The doors in the center, across from the planter, lead to service elevators and staircases. The circular areas represent the ornate fountains.

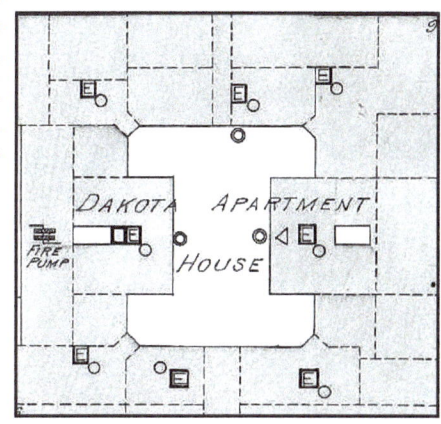

The image on the right is from a vintage map showing the buildings on and around West 72nd Street.

A PICTORIAL HISTORY

Ten

Private Restaurant

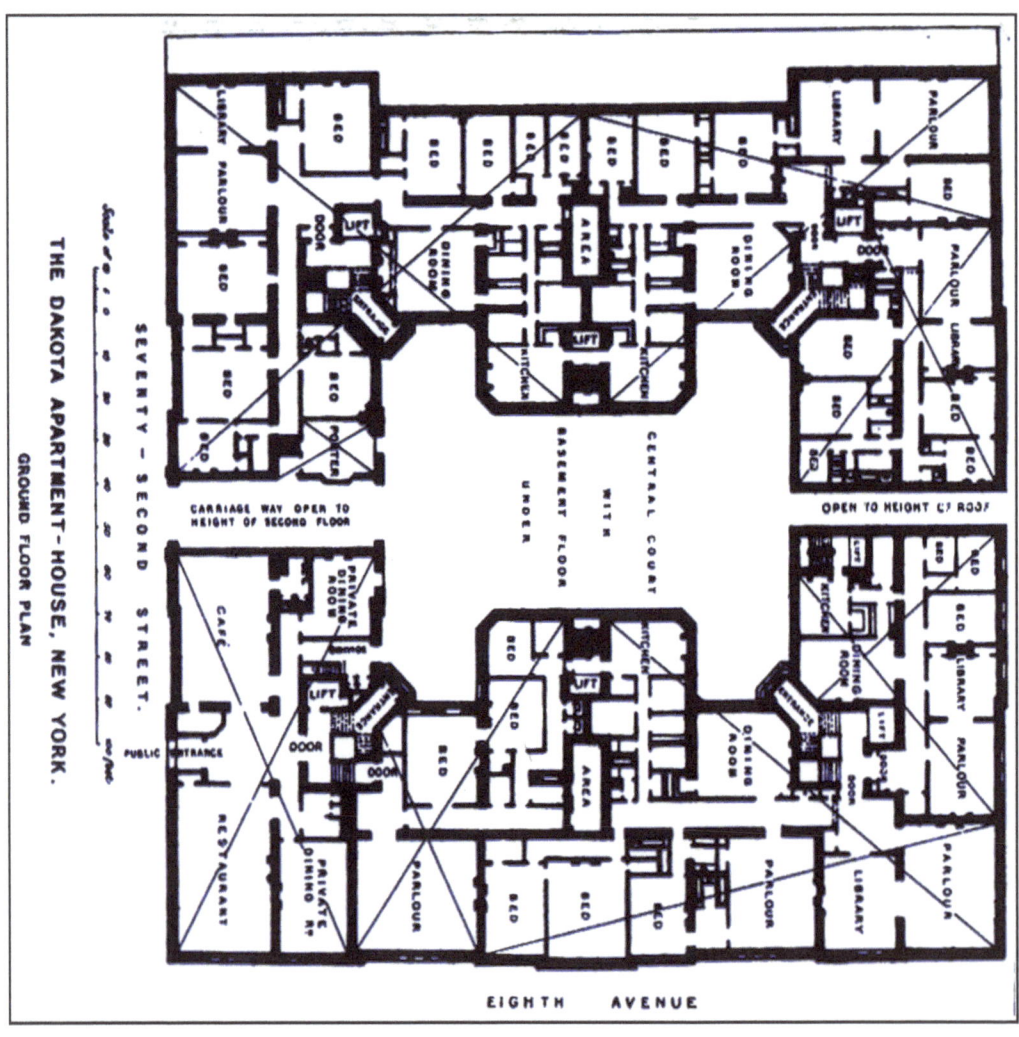

As seen in the above floorplan, during the original design stage there were plans to add an entrance on West 72nd Street directly into a public restaurant. There were plans for a cafe and two private dining rooms. The kitchen was located in the basement below and was accessed by a staircase and a lift.

THE DAKOTA

The final 1884 layout included a restaurant for residents and their guests in the southeast corner of the first floor. The large restaurant had a stone fireplace in the center, as did the smaller dining room to its west. A smaller private dining room faced Central Park. In the center was a staircase specifically designed to allow the restaurant staff to access the kitchen directly below in the basement.

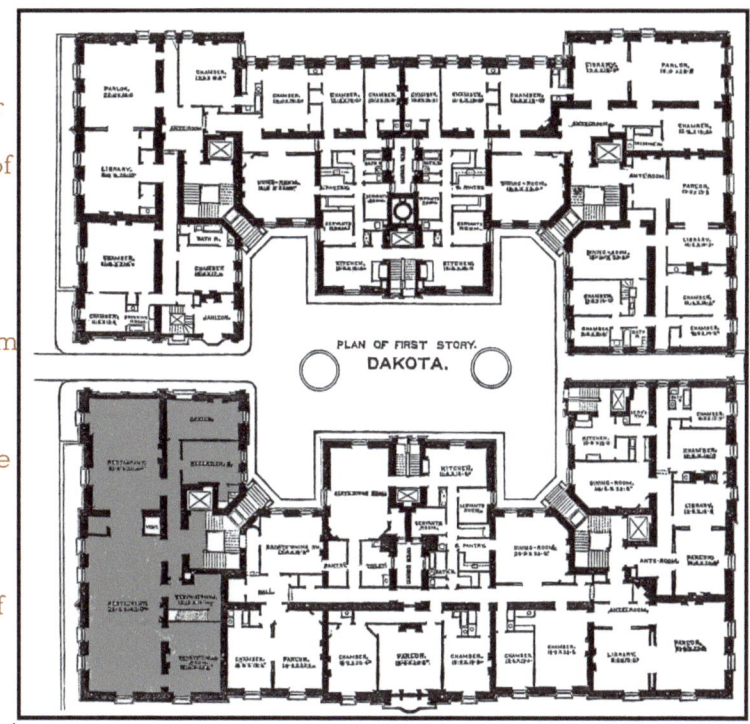

Following the conversion of the Dakota to a Co-op in 1961 the private restaurant was closed and converted into a large apartment. The main restaurant area became an enormous living room, while the private dining rooms became bedrooms. The apartment included the narrow staircase that led to the basement kitchen which was renovated to become an art studio.

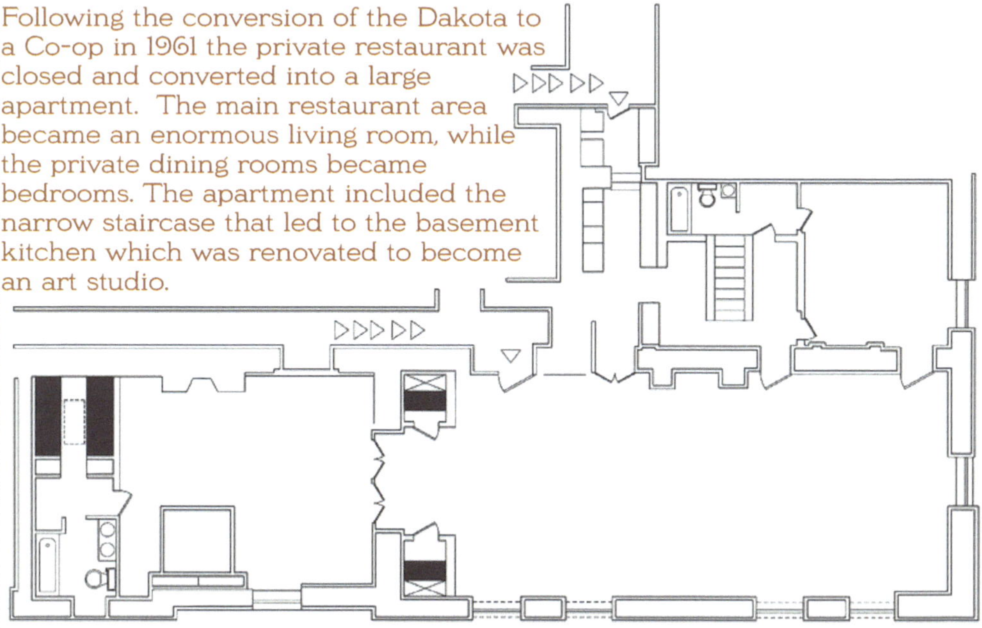

A PICTORIAL HISTORY

THE DAKOTA

Dinner

BLUE POINT OYSTERS   LITTLE NECK CLAMS

CELERY   OLIVES   RADISHES
SALTED ALMONDS   BRANDY PEACHES

GREEN TURTLE, CLEAR   CREAM OF CHICKEN
CONSOMMÉ ROYALE

BROILED POMPANO, MAITRE D'HOTEL   BOILED SALMON, SAUCE HOLLANDAISE
SLICED CUCUMBERS   POTATOES PARISIENNE

TENDERLOIN OF BEEF, LARDED, WITH FRESH MUSHROOMS
TERRAPIN A LA MARYLAND   SWEETBREADS WITH FRENCH PEAS
PEACHES WITH RICE, CONDE

RIBS OF BEEF   CAPON WITH DRESSING
VIRGINIA HAM AU MADERE

ASPARAGUS AU BEURRE   SPINACH WITH EGG   STEWED TOMATOES
NEW STRING BEANS   STEAMED RICE   BOILED BERMUDA POTATOES
MASHED POTATOES   BAKED SWEET POTATOES

CHAMPAGNE PUNCH

CANVAS-BACK DUCK WITH JELLY

LETTUCE AND TOMATO

ENGLISH PLUM PUDDING
ST. HONORE CREAM PIE   MINCE PIE   MACEDOINE JELLY
SWISS MERINGUE   PETITS FOURS   BON BONS
TUTTI FRUTTI ICE CREAM

FRUIT   ASSORTED NUTS AND RAISINS   FIGS

FOREIGN AND DOMESTIC CHEESE

COFFEE

TUESDAY, DECEMBER 25, 1900

Eleven
Courtyard

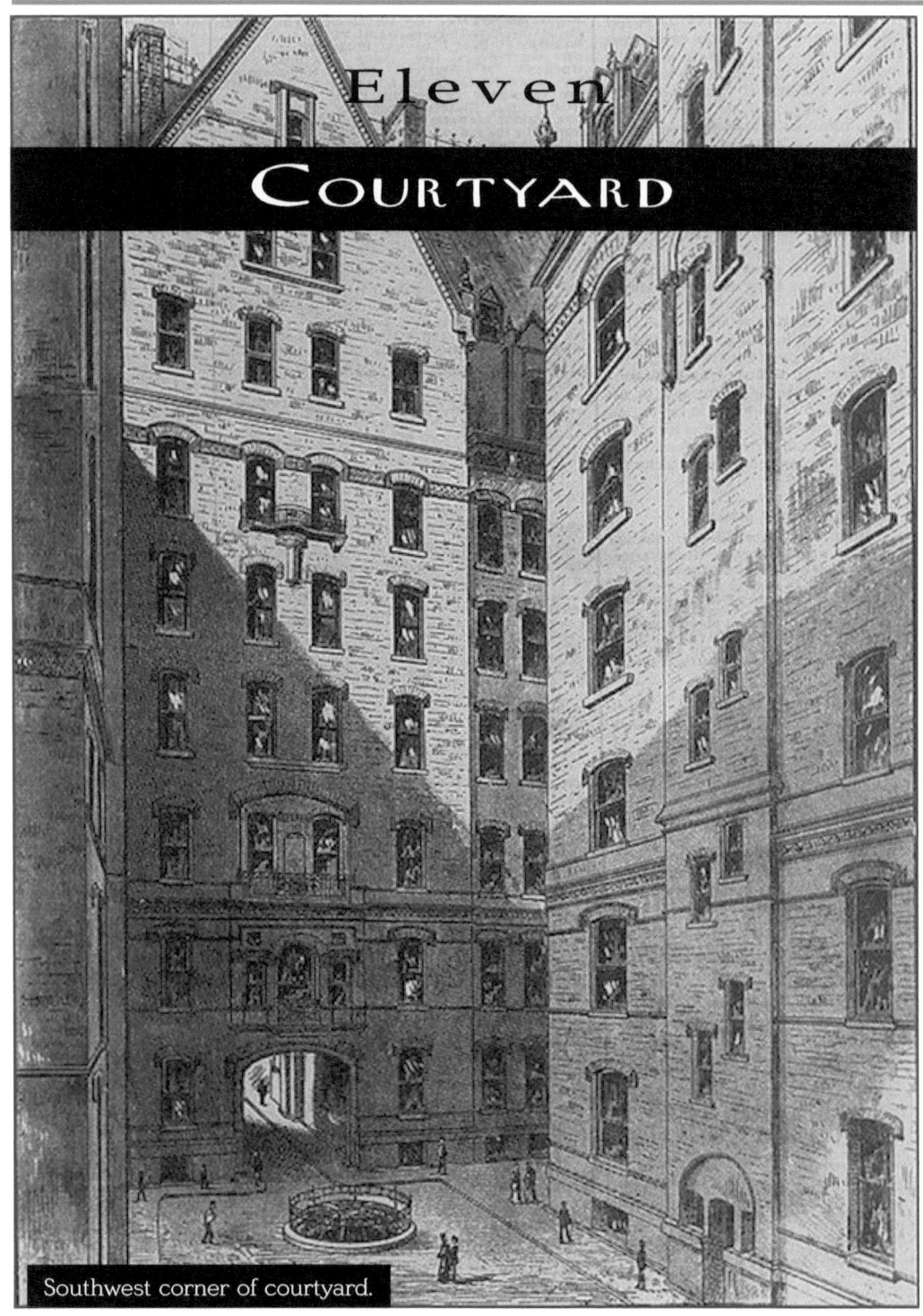

Southwest corner of courtyard.

Northeast corner of courtyard.

A PICTORIAL HISTORY

View from the southeast corner of the courtyard that allows access to the lobbies in each corner of the building.

View of southeast corner of the courtyard. The gate on the right leads to the porte-cochère. The center of the fountain has glass blocks that allows sunlight to enter the basement area below.

THE DAKOTA

The Dakota apartment building is divided into four (4) sections. This has offered residents more privacy by limiting their interaction with any residents who do not live in their section of the building. It also prevents the Dakota from having long, narrow corridors that have always been so common in large apartment buildings. In each corner of the courtyard are entries which offer immediate access to each lobby's staircase and elevator. Beneath each step are glass blocks which were designed to allow sunlight to enter through to the basement below. This was particularly helpful in the late 1800s, when electric power for residences was a new luxury.

In the center of each fountain are iron calla lilies that spout water atop cast iron panels with glass bullets. They were designed to allow sunlight to pass through them and for light to enter the basement beneath the courtyard.

A PICTORIAL HISTORY

This photo was taken from an apartment that was created in a series of attic rooms on the 8th floor. It shows a northward view of windows on 5th, 6th, and 7th floor apartments and windows on the mansard room. In the center is a breezeway above the north entry. There are iron walkways within it that allow apartments on the northwest side to access the staircase and elevators in the tower to the right of the breezeway. This design allowed Hardenbergh to avoid having to add fire escapes to the building since it offered residents in those apartments another exit in the case of an emergency.

This photo is similar to the previous one, but faces northwest and offers a better view of the grandeur of the Dakota's beautiful mansard roof. It also shows the guard rail that runs along the roof for the safety of residents who spent time on the roof for the enjoyment of the view and to appreciate cooler air in the days before air conditioning.

This photo was taken within the porte-cochère and shows the inner gate the allows entry to the beautiful courtyard. To the right is the bay window of the security office where guests must check-in before further entry.

THE DAKOTA

This photo was taken from within the Dakota's courtyard with a southward view of the porte-cochère. The above ornate iron gate guards access to the interior courtyard that can only be accessed by Dakota residents and their guests.

A PICTORIAL HISTORY

Twelve
Apartments

The Dakota has always been one of the most exclusive apartment buildings in New York. As a result, it is a unique opportunity when an apartment is put up for sale. When they are, the apartments have sometimes been purchased by such insiders as fellow Dakota residents who learn of the new properties before they are put on the market for sale by Realtors.

The below photo shows the entry door to a 7-room apt. with a 34-foot corner living room overlooking Central Park. The aptartment included a library, dining room, eat-in kitchen, butler's pantry, two bedrooms, two baths, two fireplaces, and a formal dressing room.

The above photo shows an antique-filled room in a spectacular apartment on the 2nd floor.

The photo to the right shows an east-facing room with views of Central Park. This one-of-a-kind palatial duplex had 8,337 sq. ft. with seven (7) bedrooms, four (4) woodburning fireplaces, library and a gym.

THE DAKOTA

The photo to the right shows the formal 400 sq. ft. panelled dining room within an apartment with seven (7) exquisite rooms with 14' ceilings. The apt. included original details and five (5) wood-burning fireplaces. There were two master bedrooms, each with private baths; and a third bedroom and bath. There was a spacious gourmet kitchen with a butler's pantry.

The photo to the left shows a Dakota apartment that was meticulously restored to its original condition. It included a lavish 35 x 27-foot living room, three (3) bedrooms, library, and a large family room. There were four (4) bathrooms + two (2) powder rooms, and a gourmet kitchen. It was 7,000 sq. ft. with a 1,000 sq. ft. storage room.

The photo to the right was for a spectacular apartment that included a drawing room, library, formal dining room, master suite with sauna, two additional masters connected by a small swimming pool, plus staff quarters.

A PICTORIAL HISTORY

Thirteen
EDWARD CLARK

Edward Clark.

THE DAKOTA

Edward Clark (1811 – 1882) was Isaac Singer's lawyer when he partnered with his client to form the Singer Sewing Machine Company. Along with tackling legal matters and consolodating patents, he created the installment plan in order to help people afford to buy the sewing machines. In the 1870s he began investing in real estate and became a leading developer on New York's Upper West Side.

In 1879 Edward Clark hired architect Henry J. Hardenbergh to design the Van Corlear apartments on Seventh Avenue from 55th to 56th Streets. The 6-story building, with 36 "French Flats" around an inner courtyard was an obvious precurser to the design of the Dakota.

Clark family on the steps of their home in Cooperstown, NY.

A PICTORIAL HISTORY

Fourteen
Isaac Singer

Isaac Merritt Singer was the inventor of the Singer Sewing Machine and busines partner of Edward Clark.

THE DAKOTA

 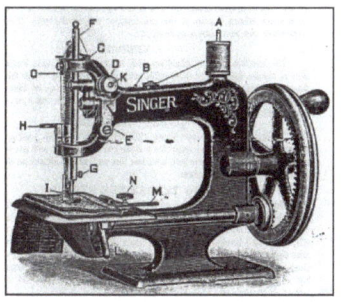 

Singer's 1851 invention could sew 900 stitches per minute. I. M. Singer & Co. manufactured 2,564 machines in 1856, and 13,000 in 1860. Singer was the first who put a family machine - "the Turtleback" - on the market. Eventually, the price dropped from $100 per machine to $10.

Located at Broadway and Liberty Street in lower Manhattan, the 47-story Singer Building was the tallest building in the world from 1908 to 1909. The building was commissioned by Frederick Bourne, the head of the Singer Sewing Machine Company. It was designed by architect Ernest Flagg.

THE SINGER MACHINE, AUGUST 12, 1851.
Earliest model filed in Patent Office. Reproduced from the SCIENTIFIC AMERICAN of November 1, 1851.

A PICTORIAL HISTORY

Fifteen
Henry Hardenbergh

Henry Janeway Hardenbergh was the architect of the Dakota.

The Plaza Hotel. 1907.

Henry Janeway Hardenbergh (1847 - 1918) was an American architect, best known for his hotels and apartment buildings.

Kirkpatrick Chapel at Rutgers College. 1873.

West 73rd Street row houses designed for Edward Clark. 1880-1881.

A PICTORIAL HISTORY

Sixteen

Residents

Steinway Family
Members of the famous piano manufacturing family were among the Dakota's first residents.

Thomas Adams' Daughters
The daughters of the man who founded the chewing gum industry shared an apartment in the Dakota.

Alfred J. Cammeyer
Retail shoe and boot merchant.

Gustav Schirmer
Founder of the American classical music publishing company.

Sir Douglas Alexander
President of the Singer Manufacturing Company from 1905–1949.

A PICTORIAL HISTORY

Frederick Ambrose Clark
American equestrian. Grandson of Edward Clark.
Brother of Edward Severin Clark.

Edward Severin Clark
Real estate developer. When his
granfather died, Edward inherited the
Dakota when he was 12 years old.

Ernest A. Gross
United States Diplomat and lawyer who
headed the U.S. delegation to the United
Nations in the lead-up to the Korean War.

Frederick Gilbert Bourne
President of the Singer Manufacturing
Company between 1889 and 1905.

THE DAKOTA

95

John Browning
Founder of The Browning School in 1888.

Henry Codman Potter
Bishop of the Episcopal Church of the United States. He was the seventh Bishop of the Episcopal Diocese of New York.

William Henry Pratt
Stage and film actor, best known for starring in film roles under the stage name Boris Karloff.

Salon J. Vlasto
Publisher of the Greek-language "Atlantic" newspaper.

A PICTORIAL HISTORY

John Lennon
English musician, singer and songwriter. He was a member of musical group The Beatles.

Leonard Bernstein
American composer, conductor, author, music lecturer and pianist.

Yoko Ono
Japanese multimedia artist, singer and peace activist.

Roberta Flack
American singer, songwriter and musician who is notable for jazz, Pop, R&B, and folk music.

Rex Reed
Film critic, book author and writer of entertainment columns for The New York Observer.

THE DAKOTA

William Inge
American playwright and novelist.

Harley Baldwin
Property developer and art dealer.

Fannie Hurst
Writer of novels, plays, screenplays,
short stories and articles

Harlan Coben
American author of mystery
novels and thrillers.

A PICTORIAL HISTORY

Marya Mannes
American author, journalist and critic.

Frederick & Anthony Victoria
Antique furniture and decorative arts dealers.

Chris Whittle
American media and education
entrepreneur. Chief Executive Officer of
"Avenues: The World School."
Former publisher of Esquire magazine.
Founder of The Edison Project.

Peter Yates
Film Director & Producer.

Charles Henri Ford
American poet, novelist, filmmaker,
photographer and collage artist.
Editor of "View" magazine.
Brother of Ruth Ford.

Joe Mielziner
American theatrical scenic designer
and lighting designer.

Judy Holliday
American actress, comedian and singer.

Syrie Maugham
British interior decorator of the
1920s and 1930s.

A PICTORIAL HISTORY

Zachary Scott
American actor

Lauren Bacall
American actress. Named the 20th greatest actress of the 20th century by the American Film Institute. Married to Jason Robards.

Gilda Radner
American comedian and actress. Original cast member of SNL.

Judy Garland
American singer, vaudevillian & actress in musical and dramatic roles.

THE DAKOTA

Ward Bennett
American designer, artist
and sculptor.

Jason Robards
American actor on stage and in film and
television.
Married to Lauren Bacall.

José Ferrer
Puerto Rican actor, theater
and film director.
Married to Rosemary Clooney.

Lillian Gish
American stage, screen and television actress,
director and writer whose film acting career
spanned 75 years, from 1912 to 1987. Gish was
called The First Lady of American Cinema.

Ted Ashley
Chairman of the
Warner Bros. film
studio from
1969 to 1980.

Albert Maysles
American documentary filmmaker.

John Brownlee
Australian operatic baritone.
Married to Countess Donna Carla
Oddone di Feletto.

Zero Mostel
American actor and comedian of
stage and screen.

John Madden
Former American football player in the NFL, a former Super Bowl-winning head coach and commentator for NFL telecasts.

Rudolf Nureyev
One of the most celebrated dancers of ballets and modern dance of the 20th century.

Connie Chung
News presenter, reporter and journalist.
Married to Maury Povich.

Maury Povich
American television presenter.
Married to Connie Chung.

A PICTORIAL HISTORY

Steven Sater
American poet, playwright, lyricist,
television writer and screenwriter.

Sidney Kingsley
American dramatist.
Married to Madge Evans.

Robert Ryan
American Actor

Ruth Ford
Model and stage and film actress.
Sister of Charles Henry Ford.

THE DAKOTA

Rosemary Clooney
Cabaret singer & actress.
Married to Jose Ferrer.

Madge Evans
Stage & Film Actress.
Married to Sidney Kingsley.

Marian Mercer
Actress and singer.

Polly Bergen
Actress, Singer, Television Host, Writer
and Entrepreneur.

A PICTORIAL HISTORY

SKETCHES OF "THE WEST END" OF NEW YORK CITY.

www.ingramcontent.com/pod-product-compliance
Lightning Source LLC
Chambersburg PA
CBHW042325150426
43192CB00004B/121